Zoo Animals

# REINDEER AT THE ZOO

By Seth Lynch

**Please visit our website, www.garethstevens.com. For a free color catalog of all our high-quality books, call toll free 1-800-542-2595 or fax 1-877-542-2596.**

**Library of Congress Cataloging-in-Publication Data**

Names: Lynch, Seth, author.
Title: Reindeer at the zoo / Seth Lynch.
Description: New York : Gareth Stevens Publishing, [2020] | Series: Zoo animals | Includes index.
Identifiers: LCCN 2018039583| ISBN 9781538239421 (paperback) | ISBN 9781538239445 (library bound) | ISBN 9781538239438 (6 pack)
Subjects: LCSH: Reindeer–Juvenile literature. | Zoo animals–Juvenile literature.
Classification: LCC QL737.U55 L96 2020 | DDC 599.65/8–dc23
LC record available at https://lccn.loc.gov/2018039583

First Edition

Published in 2020 by
**Gareth Stevens Publishing**
111 East 14th Street, Suite 349
New York, NY 10003



Editor: Therese Shea
Designer: Katelyn E. Reynolds

Photo credits: Cover, p. 1 Nadezda Nikitina/Shutterstock.com; p. 5 Theodor Negru/Shutterstock.com; p. 7 Iordache Elena G/Shutterstock.com; pp. 9, 24 (moss) Jeremy-Stenuit/Shutterstock.com; p. 11 Annettt/Shutterstock.com; p. 13 Sergey Gordienko/Shutterstock.com; pp. 15, 24 (hoof) Tagwaran/Shutterstock.com; p. 17 Bogorodskiy/Shutterstock.com; pp. 19, 24 (antler) vadimmva/Shutterstock.com; p. 21 Olenyok/Shutterstock.com; p. 23 Shestock/Blend Images/Getty Images.



Printed in the United States of America

CPSIA compliance information: Batch #CS19GS: For further information contact Gareth Stevens, New York, New York at 1-800-542-2595.

# Contents

I see reindeer
at the zoo.
I learn a lot!

Reindeer are
a kind of deer.

They eat plants.
They eat grass and moss.

They dig for food!

They have fur.
It keeps them warm.

They have hooves.
They can walk on ice.

They can swim!

They grow antlers.
Antlers are bone!

Antlers fall off
each year.
Animals eat them!

I like the reindeer
at the zoo!

# Words to Know

antler

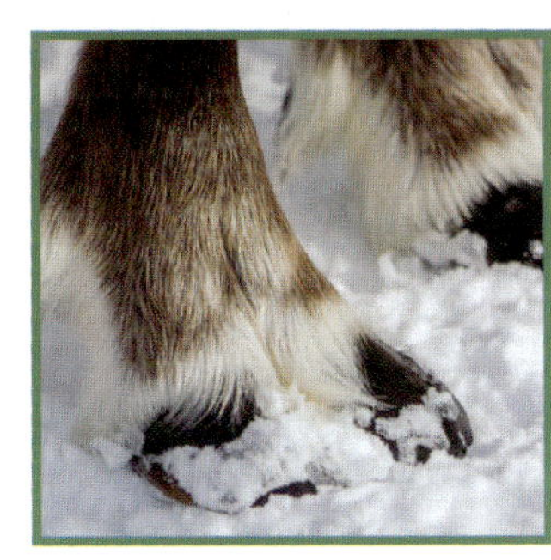
hoof

moss

# Index